My First BIG Book of SHARK FACTS

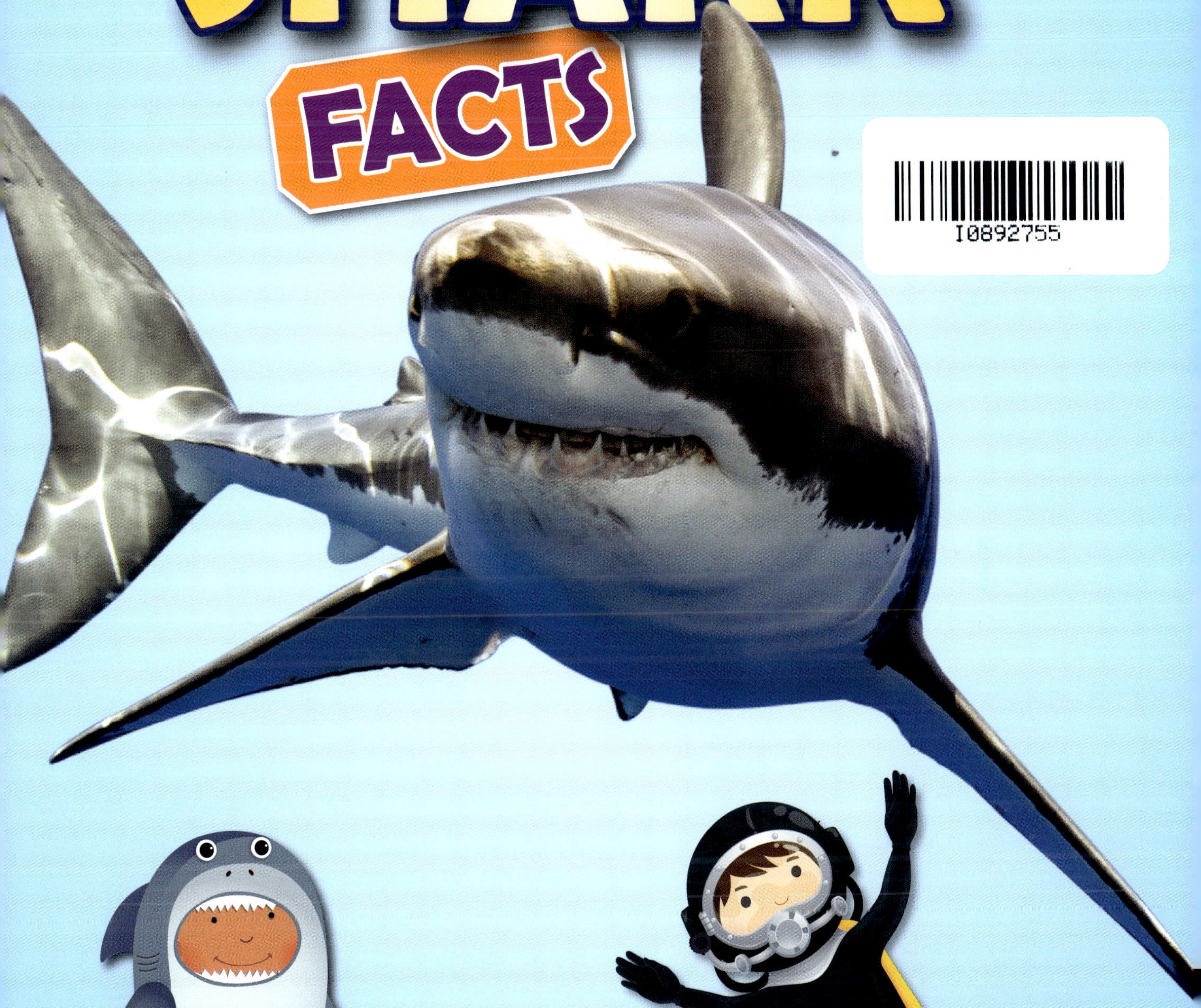

by Belinda Gallagher

Ruby Tuesday Books

Published in 2026 by Ruby Tuesday Books Ltd.

Editors: Ruth Owen & Mark J. Sachner
Design & Production: Tammy West

Photo credits:
Alamy: 6B (Kelvin Aitken/VWPics), 7TL (Mark Conlin), 7B (Auscape International PTY), 9B, 25T (Newscom), 30B (PA Images), 31B (Dorling Kindersley Ltd.), 32 (Sven Bachstrom), 35T (UPI), 41B (WaterFrame), 44B (Connect Images), 52B (ArteSub), 53 (BIOSPHOTO), 63 (Kelvin Aitken/VWPics), 66B (BIOSPHOTO), 73B (Mark Conlin), 83T (Media Drum World), 84 (WaterFrame), 86 (Scubazoo), 90T (Jeffrey Isaac Greenberg), 91T (Zuma Press Inc); Blue Planet Archive LLC (Alamy): 39C, 51, 64B; Chris & Monique Fallows (Nature Picture Library): 26T, 50T, 50B, 87B; Jason Kominsky: 33B, 37T; James Kuether: 31T, 33T, 36, 37B; Andy Murch (Nature Picture Library): 43, 61BR, 64T, 67; Alex Mustard (Nature Picture Library): 4–5, 58B, 69; Nature Picture Library: 5T (Alex Hyde), 21T (David Fleetham), 38T (Cheryl-Samantha Owen), 56B (Brandon Cole), 57 (Brian Skerry), 60T (Pascal Kobeh), 66TL (David Shale), 68 (Franco Banfi), 71B (Ralph Pace), 74–75 (Shane Gross), 76B (Brian Skerry), 80T (Brian Skerry), 80B (Pete Oxford), 81T (Pete Oxford); Doug Perrine (Alamy/Nature Picture Library): 19T, 42, 54T, 65T, 70, 76T; Jeff Rotman (Alamy/Nature Picture Library): 16T, 48T, 49B, 81B; Science Photo Library: 10–11 (3DMEDISPHERE), 47B (UCL, Grant Museum of Zoology); Shutterstock: Cover (Nicolas-SB/W.Scott McGill), 1, 6T, 8, 9, 11, 12–13, 13, 14, 15, 17, 18T, 19B, 20, 21B, 22, 23, 24, 25B, 26B, 27, 28, 29, 30T, 33T, 34, 35B, 38B, 39T, 39B, 40, 41T, 44T, 45B, 46, 47T, 48B, 49T, 52T, 54B, 55, 56T, 58T, 58–59, 59B, 60B, 61T, 61BL, 62, 65T, 65B, 66TR, 71T, 72, 73T, 74, 77, 78, 79, 82, 83B, 85, 87T, 88, 89, 90B (for a full detailed list of contributors, contact info@rubytuesdaybooks.com); Superstock: 7TR (Jeff Rotman).

Library of Congress Control Number: 2024948190

Print (Hardback) ISBN 978-1-78856-513-4
Print (Paperback) ISBN 978-1-78856-514-1
ePub ISBN 978-1-78856-515-8

Published in Minneapolis, MN
Printed in the United States

www.rubytuesdaybooks.com

What's Inside?

What Is a Shark?

Sharks are fish that live in oceans. They are excellent swimmers and hunt other animals to eat.

All sharks have tails, **fins**, and **gills**.

A shark's skin is covered with tiny spikes called **denticles**.

They help the shark slide easily through water.

This is a close-up picture of shark skin.

Water slips easily off smooth denticles.

Great white shark

Most sharks have sharp teeth. But not all do!

Scientists have discovered more than 500 different kinds of sharks.

There could still be new sharks to discover.

No, they don't! Sharks have differently shaped bodies. They can be big, small, and even flat, like this angelshark.

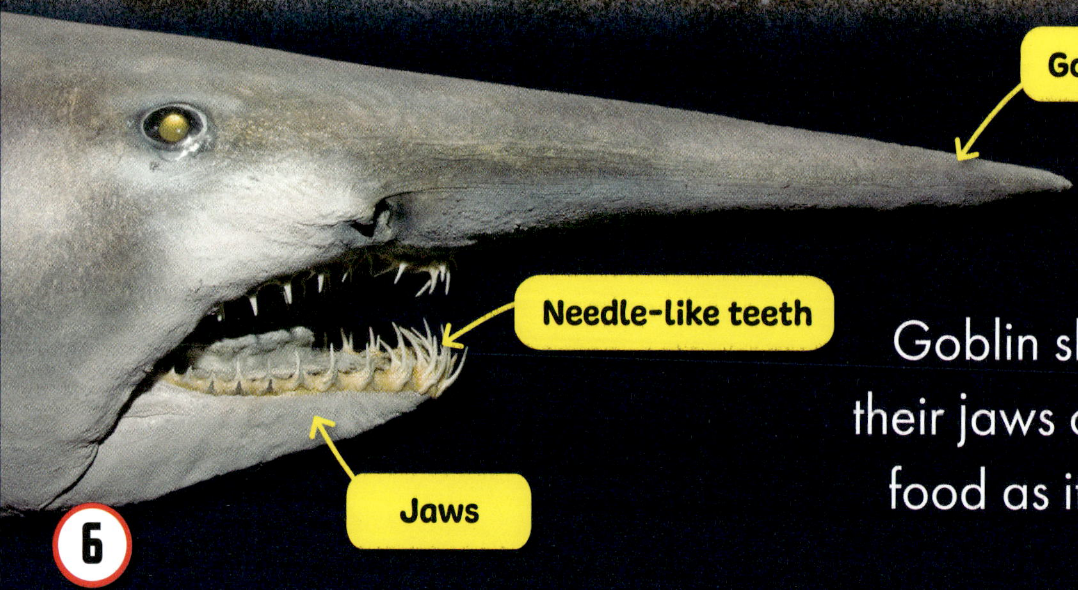

Goblin sharks push their jaws out to snatch food as it swims by.

Horn sharks have sharp spines that tell other animals to stay away!

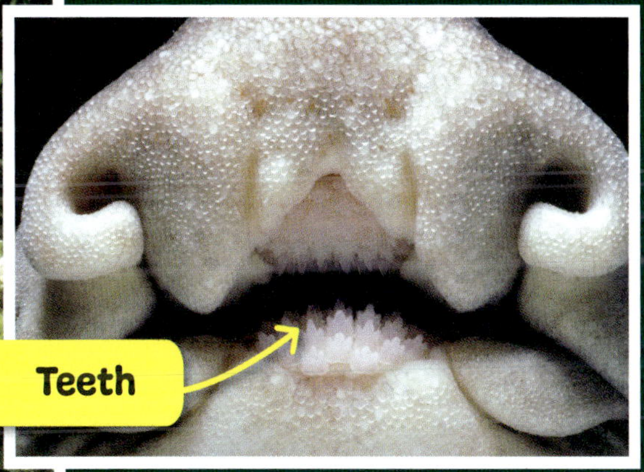

A horn shark has tiny teeth.

This longnose sawshark has a saw-like snout for finding **prey** on the seabed.

How Do Scientists Group Sharks?

There are hundreds of different types of sharks. Scientists sort them into eight groups.

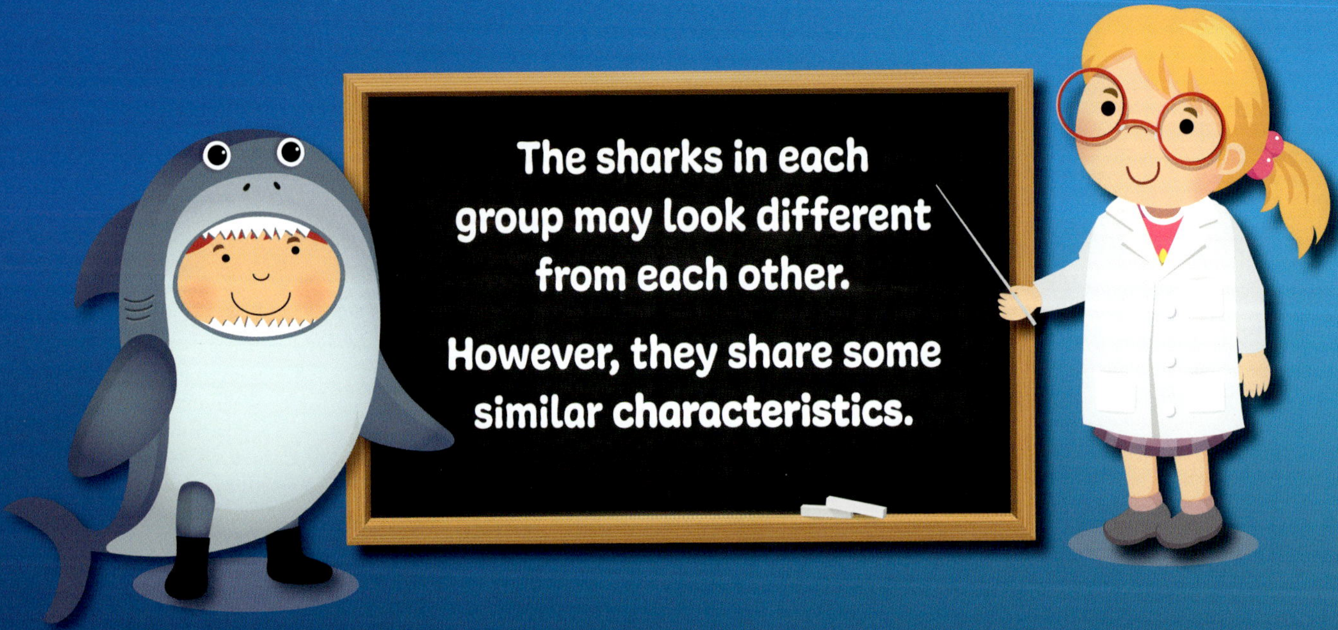

Mackerel sharks

These sharks have big mouths with several rows of teeth.

Some feed on tiny **plankton**. Others are fierce hunters.

Ground sharks

This group is the biggest group.

They have eyelids that move and sharp teeth.

Carpet sharks

These sharks have skin patterns that look like carpets or rugs!

Dogfish sharks

Sharks in this group hunt and feed in packs, like wild dogs.

Cow and frilled sharks

These sharks have six or seven gill slits.

Sharks in this group first lived on Earth before the dinosaurs.

Angel sharks

Sharks in this group have flat bodies.

Their body shape and skin patterns help them hide in sand to catch their prey.

Bullhead sharks

Sawsharks

Why Don't Sharks Have Bones?

All sharks have a skeleton. But instead of hard bone, it is made of a bendy material called cartilage.

Cartilage is lighter than bone.

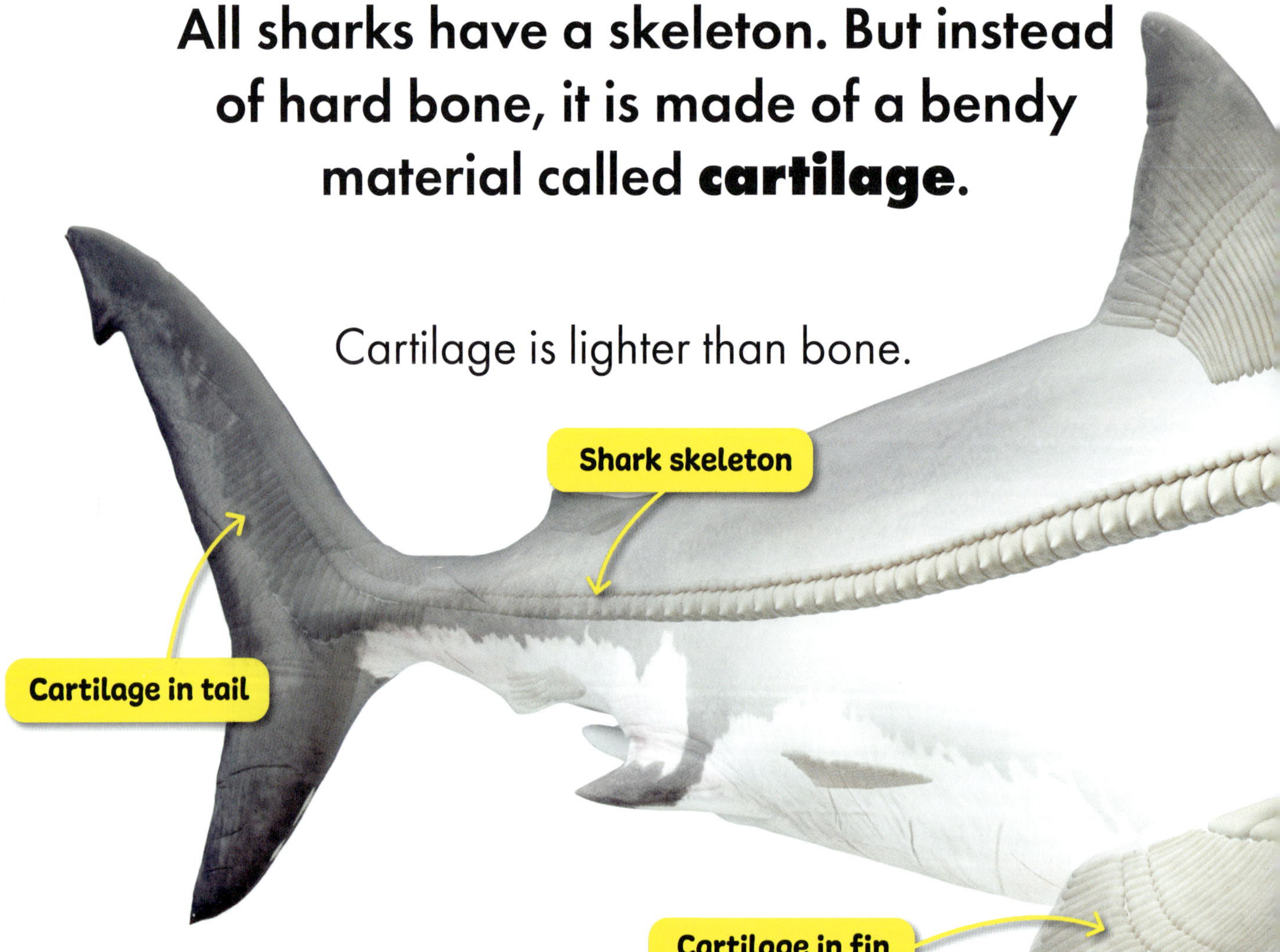

Sharks need to twist and turn quickly to catch food.

A bendy skeleton is useful for this.

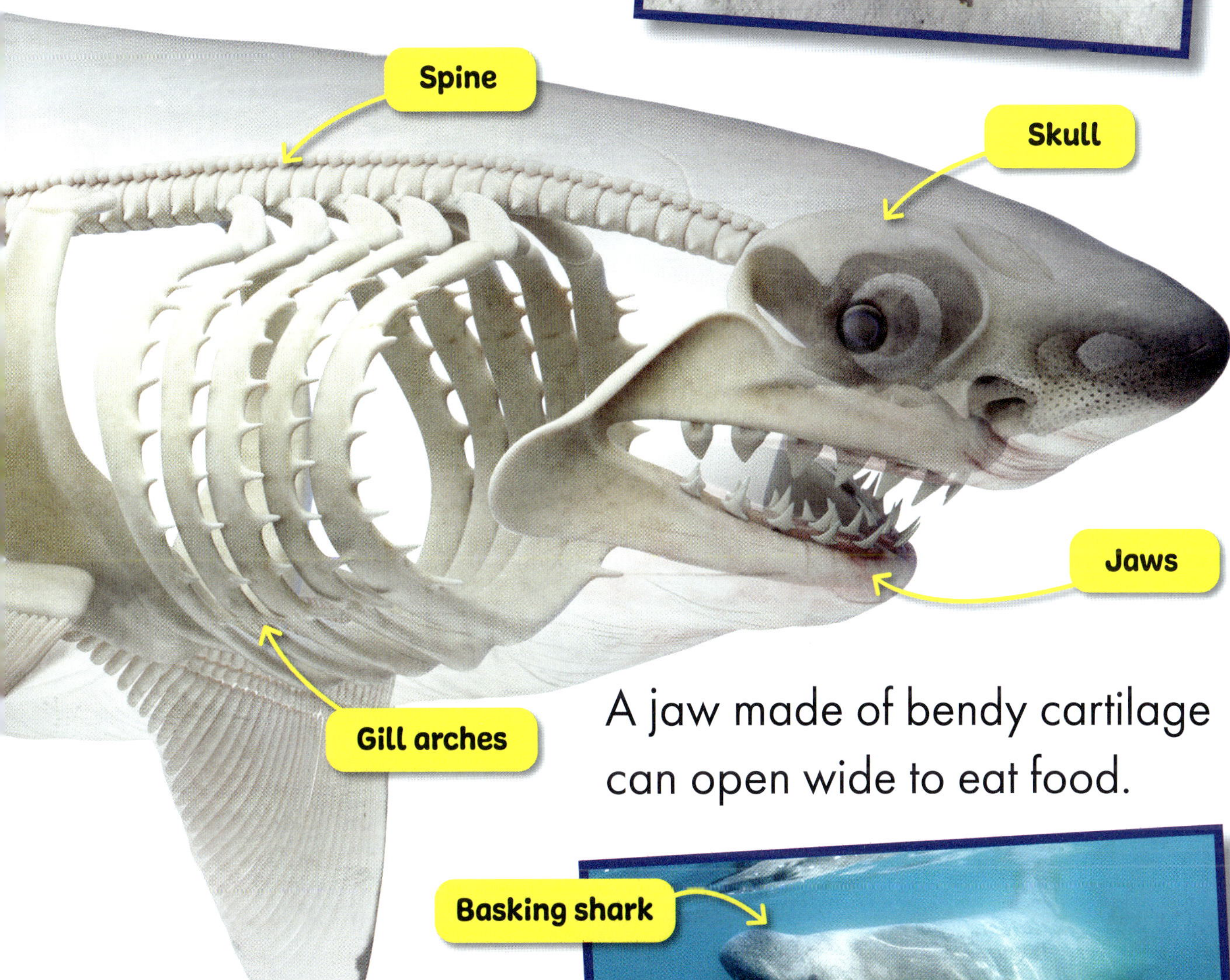

A jaw made of bendy cartilage can open wide to eat food.

Basking sharks can open their jaws wider than any other shark!

How Do Sharks Swim So Fast?

Shark bodies are streamlined. This means the water flows smoothly around them.

They have strong muscles and a light, bendy skeleton.

A shark's tail flicks from side to side to push through the water.

Fins help a shark balance and change direction.

Most sharks have eight fins.

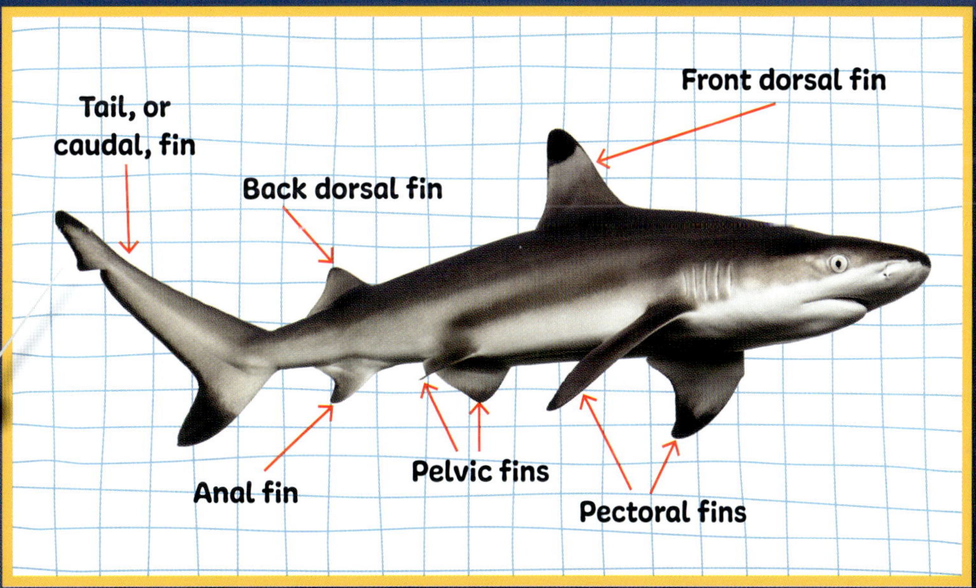

How Do Sharks Breathe Underwater?

Like all animals, sharks need a gas called oxygen to survive.

Water flows into a shark's mouth and over its gills.

The gills take oxygen from the water.

The shark's heart pumps the oxygen around its body.

An epaulette shark can survive for up to one hour without oxygen!

It hunts in shallow tide pools where there is little oxygen.

Do Sharks Have Good Eyesight?

Water can be dark and murky, so most sharks have good eyesight.

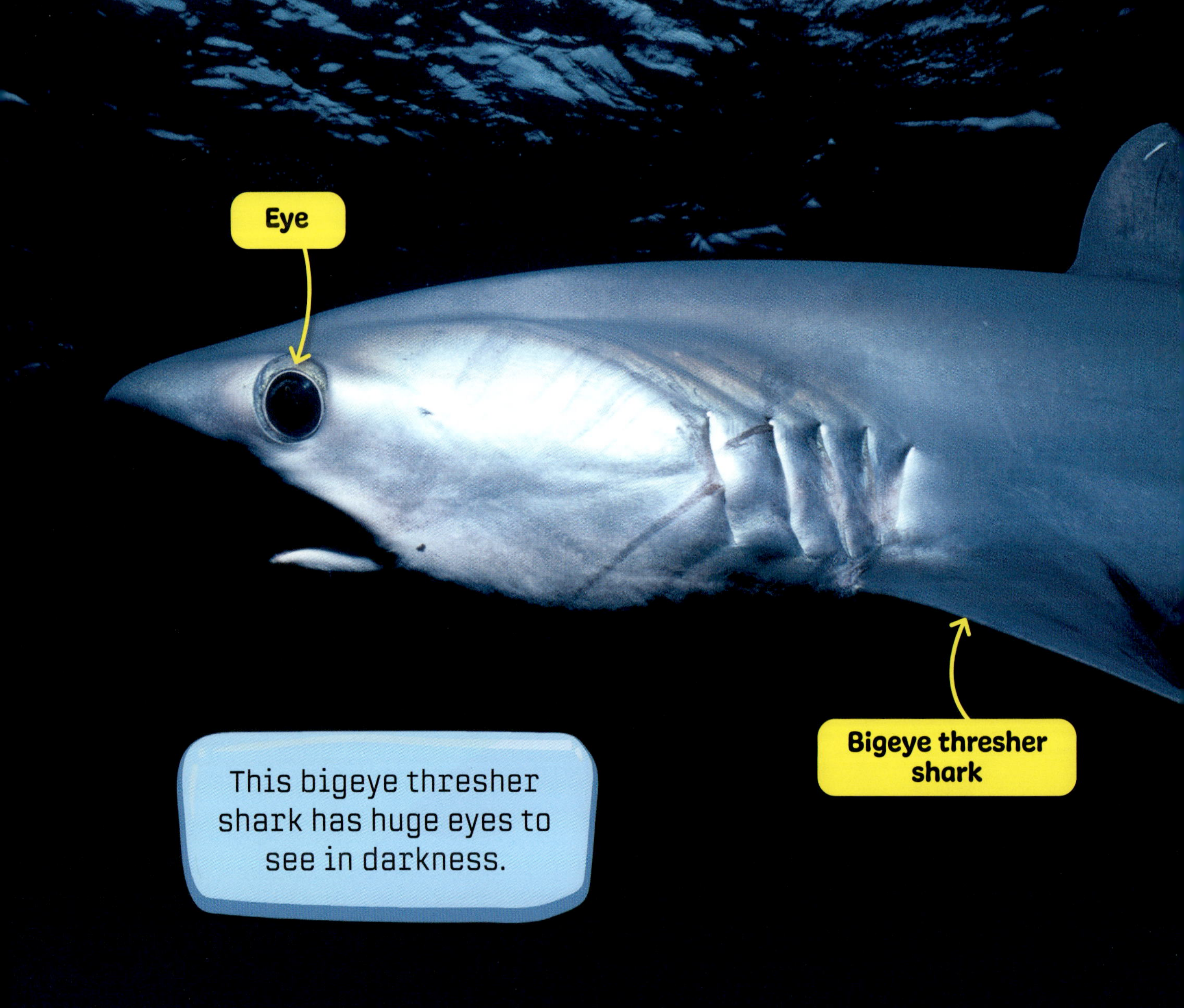

This bigeye thresher shark has huge eyes to see in darkness.

Many sharks hunt at night, so they must see well in the dark.

This great white shark is "spyhopping."

It wants to see what's happening above the water.

Hammerhead sharks have an eye on each end of their hammer-like head.

They sweep their heads from side to side to look for their prey.

Are Sharks Cold-Blooded or Warm-Blooded?

Most sharks, such as this tiger shark, are **cold-blooded**.

This means the shark's body temperature changes to match how cold or warm the water is around it.

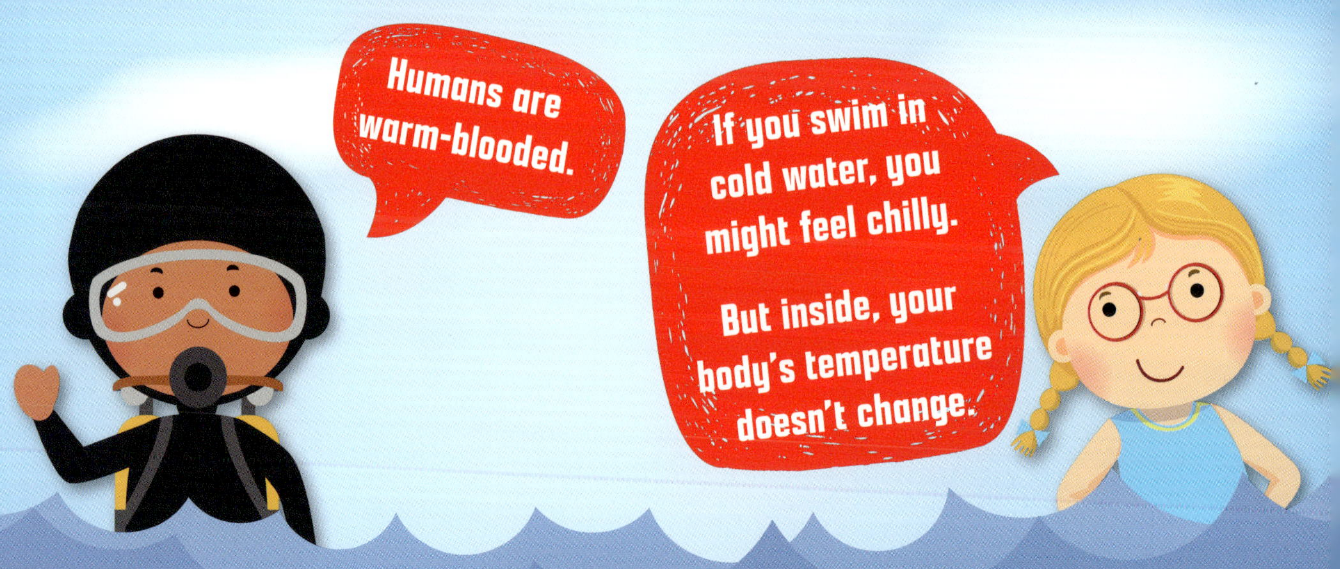

Some sharks can warm up parts of their bodies.

A salmon shark has a body temperature warmer than the water.

This helps it swim quickly to catch fast-moving salmon.

A great white shark can also warm up its muscles.

Then it can attack prey with power and speed.

Who Hitches a Ride on Sharks?

Small fish called remoras stick to sharks. They get a free ride—and free food!

A remora eats pesky **parasites** that live on shark skin.

This keeps a shark clean and healthy.

A remora has a sucker on its head that sticks to the shark.

Some fish are brave enough to clean a shark's teeth and gills!

They eat pieces of food and parasites.

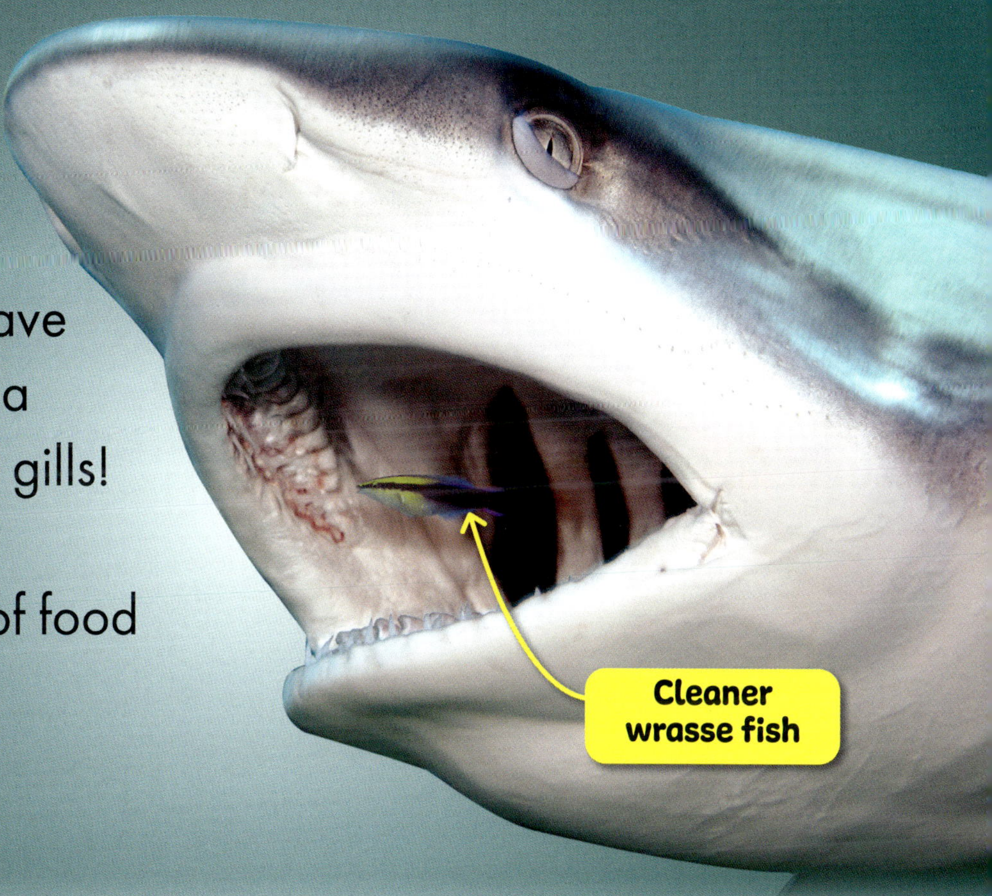

Pilot fish swim close to sharks.

They keep safe from **predators** and get to eat scraps of shark food.

Why Do Sharks Have Pointed Teeth?

Sharks have sharp, pointed teeth for catching and eating food.

A sand tiger, or ragged tooth, shark has thin, needle-like teeth for grabbing small fish.

A Port Jackson shark has small, sharp teeth. These teeth catch animals such as crabs, clams, and sea urchins.

Large, jagged teeth are just right for eating bigger prey, such as seals.

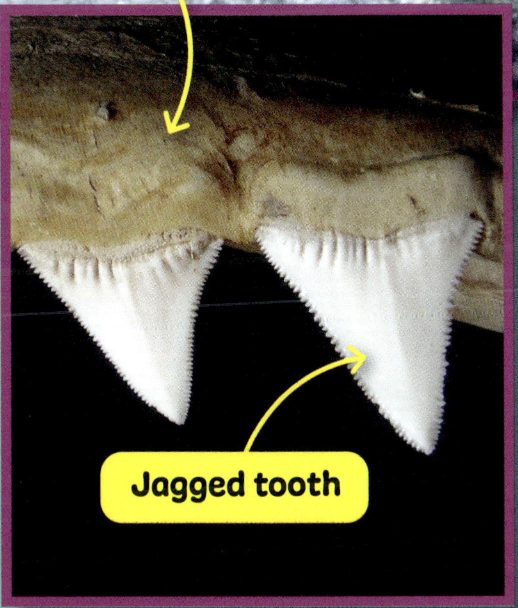

Great white shark teeth

A shark's teeth may fall out.

Then the old teeth are replaced by new ones growing in its jaws.

Are All Sharks Meat-Eaters?

Yes. All sharks are meat-eaters, or carnivores. Most sharks eat fish—including other sharks!

Sharks also eat seabirds and sea mammals, such as seals.

Some sharks get very excited when they eat.

They may whoosh up the sand to find food and even fight each other!

This is called a feeding frenzy.

Sharks swallow their food whole without chewing.

The biggest sharks eat tiny food called plankton.

A model of a megamouth shark

A megamouth shark feeds on plankton called krill.

Plankton includes mini animals, such as krill, and plant-like living things.

How Do Sharks Hunt?

Sharks are top hunters in the ocean.

Some sharks work as a team to trap fast-moving fish.

A thresher shark uses its extra-long tail fin to herd fish into a bait ball.

Then it whacks the fish with its tail!

Other sharks blend in with their **coral reef** home.

They hide and wait for their prey—then they

ATTACK!

A wobbegong shark

Do Sharks Have Superpowers?

Sharks have incredible senses that help them figure out the world around them.

HEARING
A shark can hear prey moving or splashing up to half a mile away.

SIGHT
Most sharks have special shiny parts in their eyes. This helps them hunt in dark water. Eyes on the sides of its head let a shark see in all directions.

SMELL
A shark can smell tiny amounts of blood in the water—up to a quarter of a mile away. This helps a hungry shark find injured animals to eat.

SUPER SNOUT

All living things give off electrical signals. A shark detects these signals with tiny, jelly-filled pits, or holes, on its snout. A shark's super snout helps it hunt in darkness or find prey hidden in sand.

How Long Have Sharks Been Around?

Sharks have lived on Earth for 450 million years.

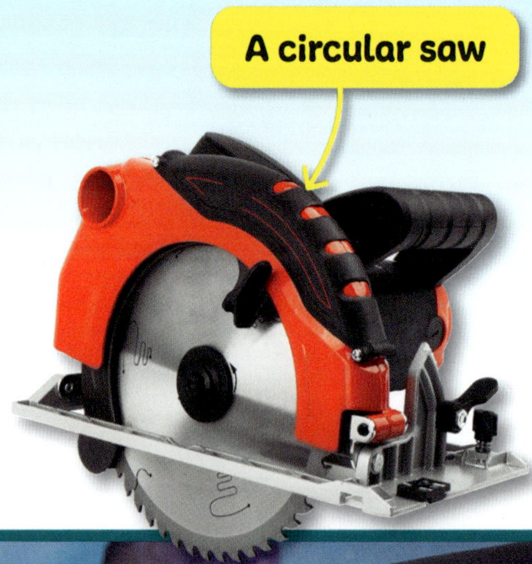

A Helicoprion shark had sharp teeth that looked like a saw!

A Stethacanthus had a flat-topped fin with spiky denticles.

Some scientists think male sharks had this special fin to show off to females!

Stethacanthus lived 370 million years ago.

A Hybodus shark had long, pointed spines on its fins.

Hybodus lived 250 million years ago.

The spines probably made this shark very difficult to eat.

Which Shark Is the Biggest of All Time?

The biggest shark of all time was the prehistoric Megalodon.

This huge, fierce hunter was the top predator of its time.

It became **extinct** about 3.6 million years ago.

Megalodon makes today's great white shark seem small.

Megalodon was as long as two school buses.

It was as heavy as 10 elephants.

Fossil bones from Megalodon's backbone have been found.

They are the size of dinner plates!

How Big Were Megalodon's Teeth?

A Megalodon's tooth is bigger than your hand. In fact, its name means "Big Tooth."

Fossil Megalodon teeth have been found all over the world.

Scientists compared Megalodon teeth to great white shark teeth.

This helped them figure out how **big** Megalodon was!

Megalodon had more than 200 teeth in its jaws.

They grew in several rows.

Megalodon's teeth were razor-sharp with jagged edges.

What Did Megalodon Hunt?

A mega-shark needed plenty of food. Its favorite prey was whales. Big prey meant more meat!

It may have used a burst of speed to surprise its prey.

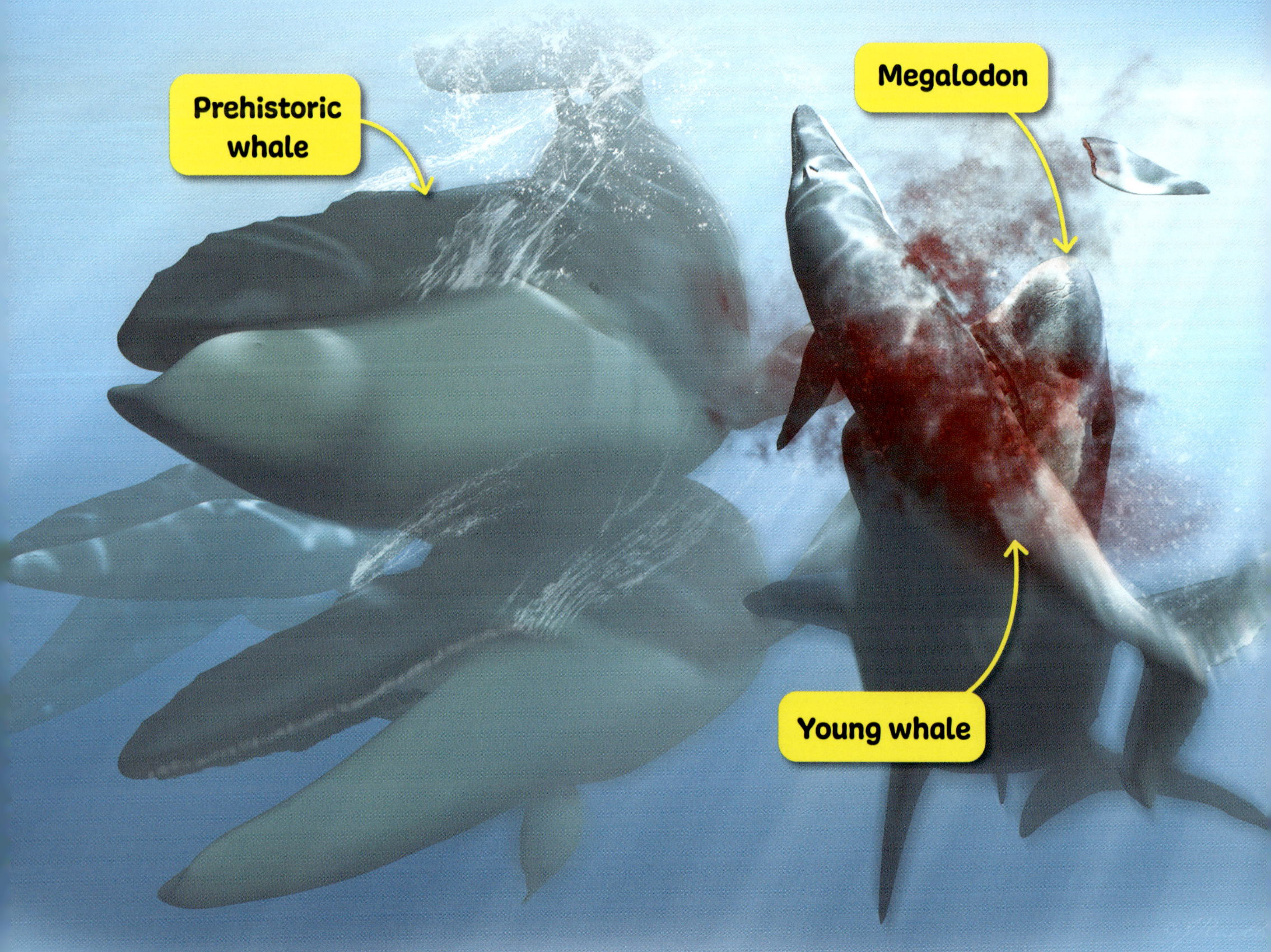

Megalodon also hunted prehistoric dolphins, seals, turtles—almost anything it could find.

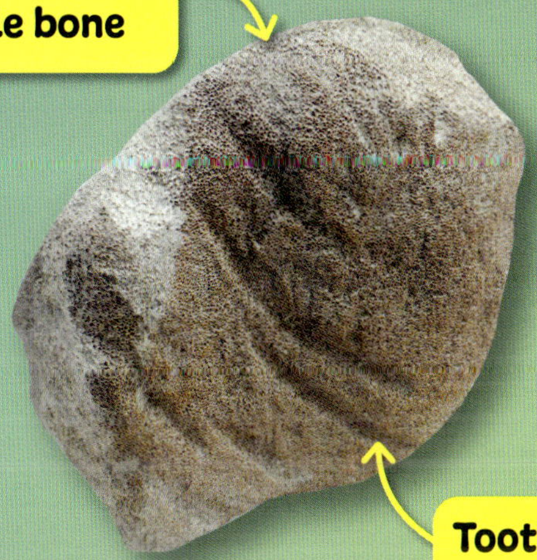

Megalodon's bite could crush big bones.

This fossil whale bone has Megalodon tooth marks on it!

Megalodon's bite may have been the strongest of any animal that ever lived.

Even stronger than a Tyrannosaurus rex!

Where Do Sharks Live and Hunt?

The ocean has lots of different **habitats** that are just right for sharks.

A feeding frenzy in shallow water

Some sharks hunt in warm, shallow seas that are packed with prey.

This zebra shark hunts for crunchy crustaceans on the sandy, rocky seabed.

Seagrass meadows provide ocean animals with lots of food and shelter.

THIS ATTRACTS SHARKS!

Sharks visit this habitat to hunt fish, plus plant-eating turtles and dugongs.

Who Hangs Out in the Coral?

A coral reef is a habitat that's home to sharks, fish, and many other ocean animals.

Fish swim among the coral in big groups called schools.

Reef sharks hide in the coral to keep safe from bigger sharks.

Coral reefs are also safe places where baby sharks can hide from bigger sharks.

Many sharks hunt at night. It's harder for their prey to spot them.

Who Lives in Icy Waters?

The Greenland shark lives in the icy Arctic Ocean—near the North Pole!

This big, slow-swimming shark can live for more than 400 years!

Salmon sharks are fierce cold-water hunters.

This is where they find their favorite salmon prey.

Sleeper sharks move slowly through cold waters.

They suck up their prey, such as octopuses, squid, fish, and crabs.

Do Sharks Live in Deep Water?

Some sharks can swim in deep, cold water. But most stay in warmer, sunlit water.

This shark has seven gills to take in more oxygen in deep water.

Blue sharks hunt for prey in cold, deep water.

Then they swim to the surface to warm up.

The Portuguese dogfish lives deeper than any other shark. It lives at almost 11,500 feet (3,500 m) down!

The ocean is divided into zones.

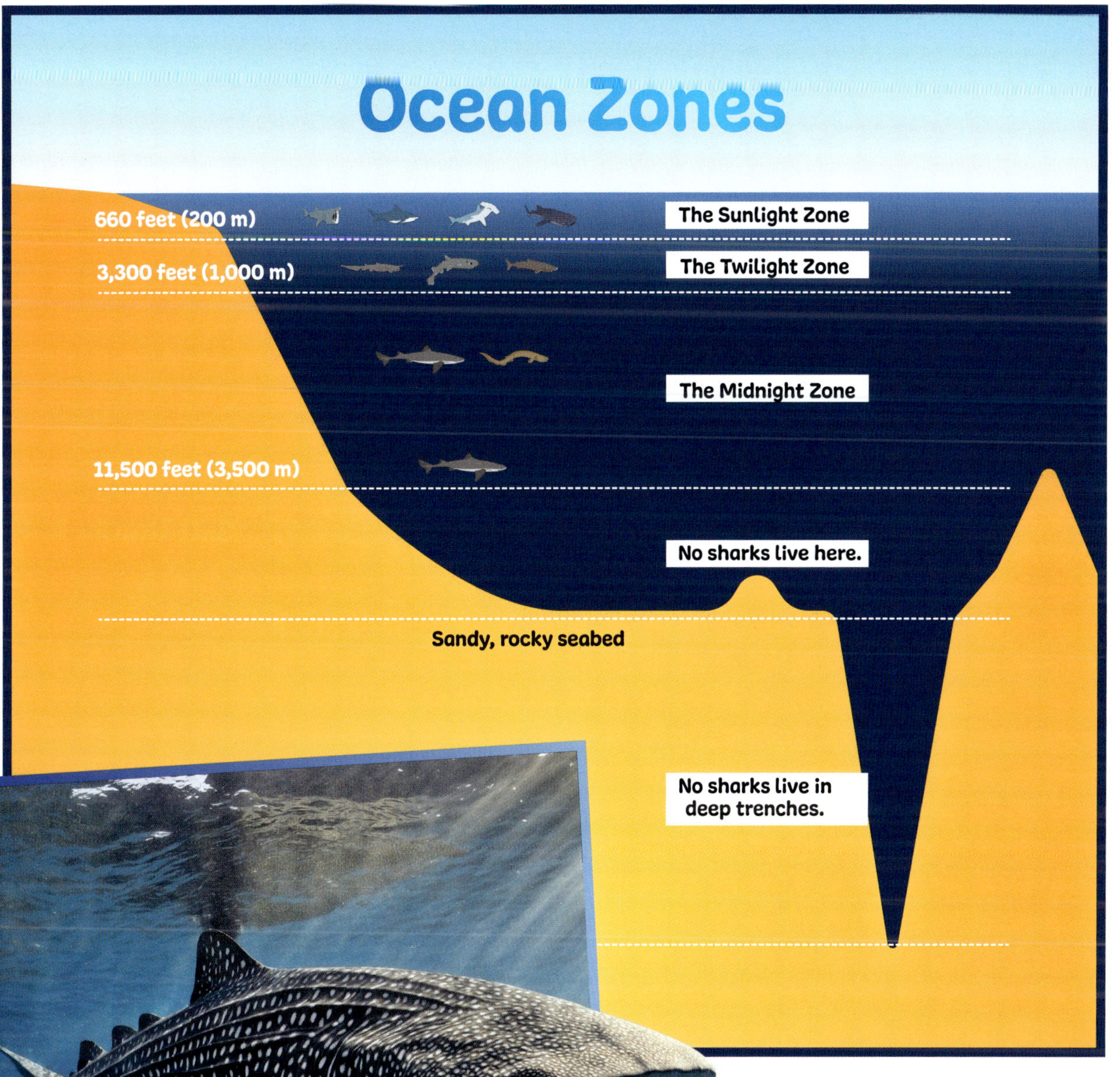

A whale shark in the sunlight zone

The deeper the water, the less light there is.

Most sharks and lots of other animals live in the sunlight zone.

This zone is packed with food.

Do Sharks Live in Rivers?

Yes! In fact, bull sharks are sometimes called "river sharks."

Bull sharks can live in salty ocean water and in freshwater.

Sometimes they swim from the sea into rivers.

Bull sharks bump their prey with their big heads. Then they bite!

A bull shark may have 350 teeth in its mouth.

Which Shark Is the Greatest?

We think it's the most famous shark of all—the great white shark!

It's the biggest hunting fish in the world.

Great white shark

A great white has more than 300 jagged teeth for slicing through prey.

A great white's colors help it hid from its prey and from orcas that may attack it.

Its gray back blends in with the water.

Its white belly makes it hard to see against the bright surface of the water.

How Does a Great White Shark Catch a Seal?

To catch speedy seals, a great white shark must surprise them.

It uses speed and strength to attack.

A great white shark

The shark is so powerful, it can jump out of the water!

Before it attacks, the shark rolls its eyes back.

This protects its eyes from struggling prey.

A dead whale also makes a good meal for a great white.

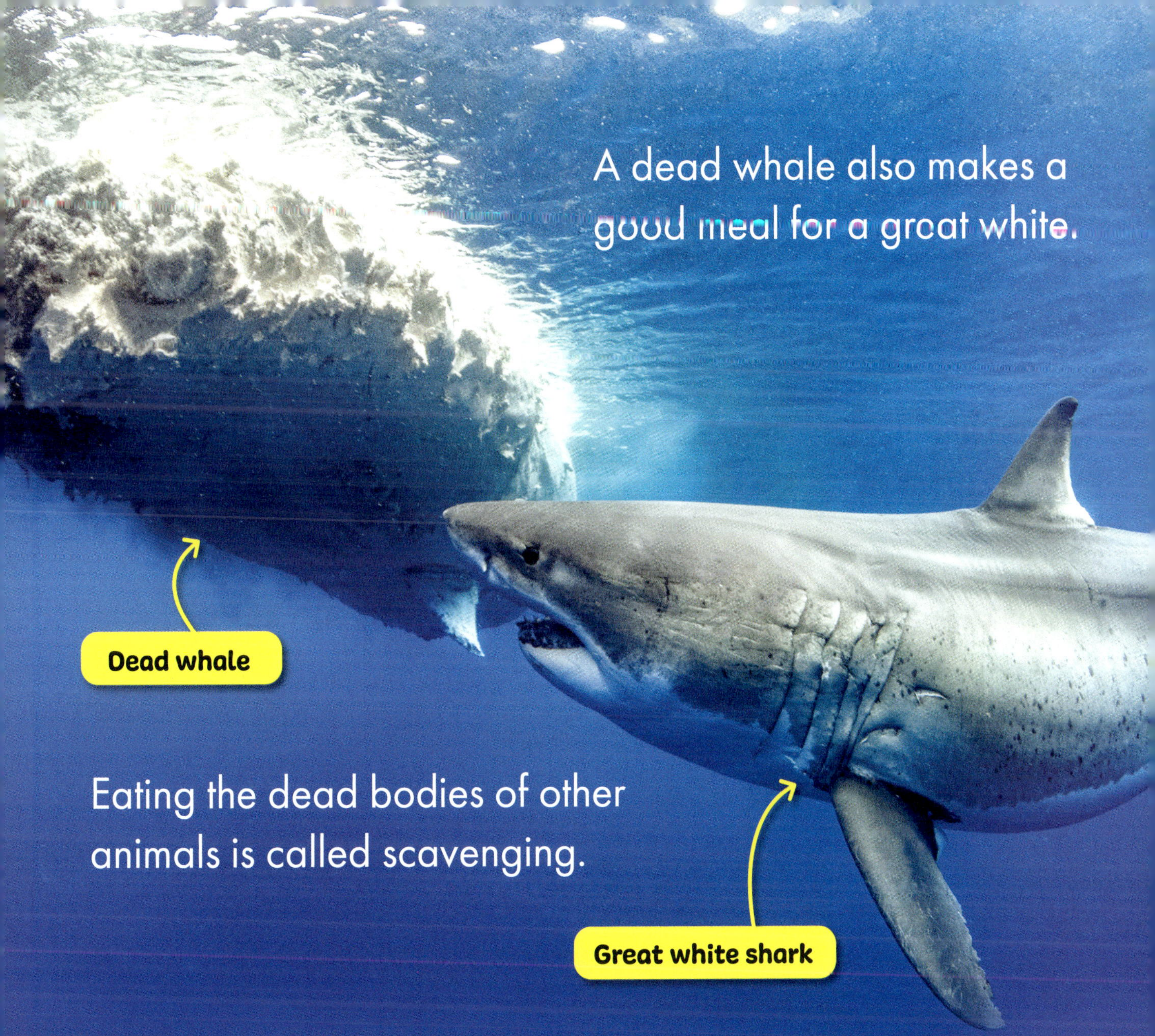

Eating the dead bodies of other animals is called scavenging.

Which Shark Will Eat Anything?

Tiger sharks are not fussy. These fierce hunters eat almost anything they can find!

Young birds that are learning to fly often become a tiger shark's snack.

A tiger shark can live for up to 50 years. The pattern on its body fades as it gets older.

Tiger sharks are clean-up sharks!

They eat dead animals, like this whale.

By eating dead animals, sharks help keep the ocean clean.

Which Sharks Are Gentle Giants?

Whale sharks and basking sharks are gentle giants.

They are known as **filter** feeders because they filter their food from the sea.

A huge basking shark swims at the surface with its mouth open.

Water flows into the shark's mouth.

Special parts called gill rakers trap plankton.

Whale sharks also filter plankton and tiny fish from the water.

How Big Is a Whale Shark?

It can be the size of a school bus!

This huge shark is the biggest fish in the ocean.

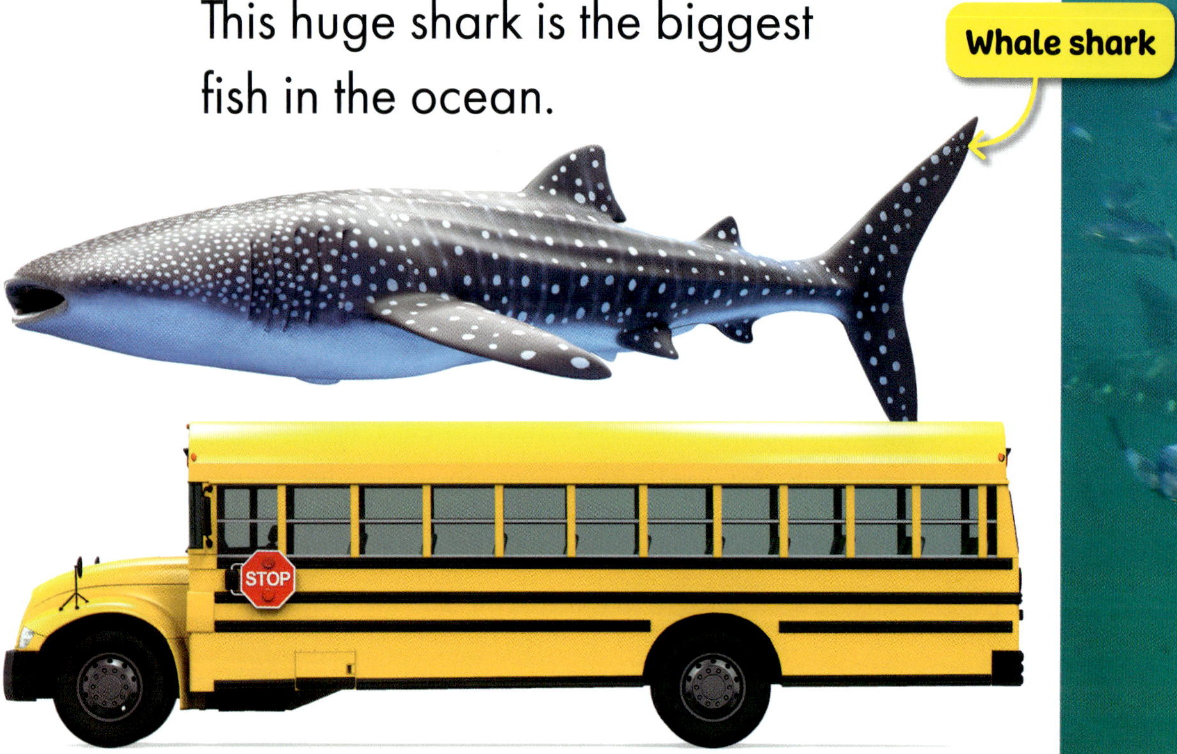

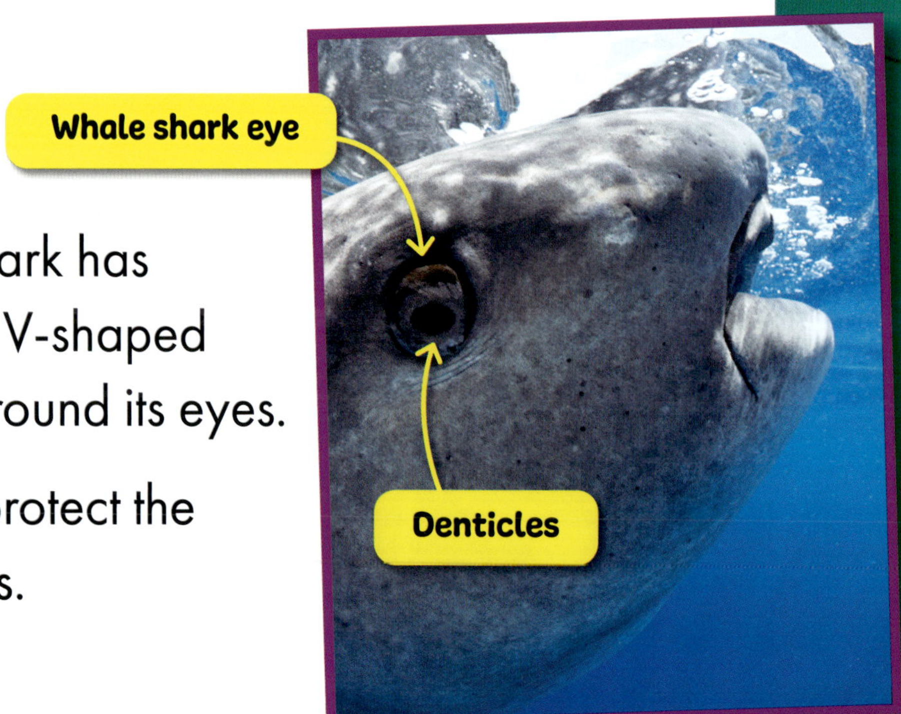

A whale shark has tiny, sharp, V-shaped denticles around its eyes.

They help protect the shark's eyes.

Whale sharks have the thickest skin of any animal.

Whale sharks are so gentle, scientists can safely swim with them.

Few animals would attack an adult whale shark.

Their biggest danger comes from **pollution** and hunting by humans.

Which Sharks Have Hammers for Heads?

The hammerheads, of course!

Hammerheads often swim in large groups called schools.

There are nine types of hammerhead sharks. The biggest is the great hammerhead.

It can grow to 20 feet (6 m) long.

A hammerhead has an eye at each end of its head for seeing all around.

Hammerheads hunt fish, squid, and stingrays that hide in sand.

The shark uses its flat head to pin a stingray to the seabed.

Do Sharks Have Spots?

Yes! Some sharks have spots and other patterns on their skin.

A puffadder shyshark's pattern helps it hide in coral reefs and seaweed.

The shark gets its name from its stripes and spots.

They look like a puffadder snake's pattern.

This wobbegong's skin tassels and patterns help it hide from predators and prey.

A leopard catshark has a beautiful skin pattern like a leopard's fur.

Who Hides in the Sand?

**Angel sharks do!
They cover their flat bodies
with sand on the seabed.**

They have eyes on top of their heads.

This helps them spot passing prey.

The fish doesn't see the hiding shark until it's too late.

The angel shark bursts from the sand!

The shark's needle-sharp teeth make it impossible for the fish to escape.

in the Dark?

Yes. Some sharks can light up in deep, dark water.

Lantern sharks glow to attract prey and scare away predators.

This pencil-sized cookiecutter shark lights up to attract big animals.

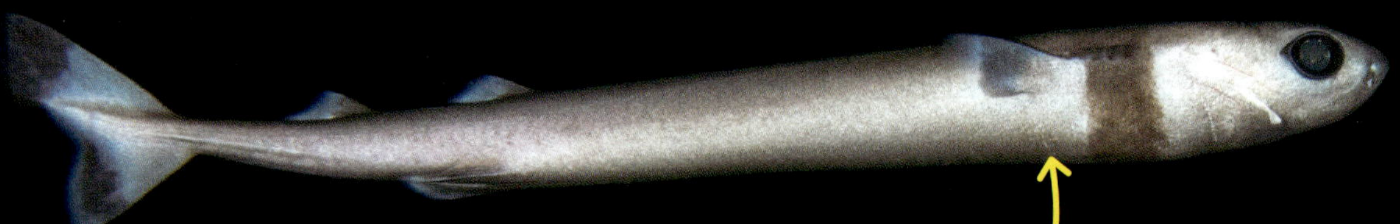

When animals make light, it's called bioluminescence.

Let's say it! Bi-oh-loo-mi-ne-scence

The tiny cookiecutter shark bites a chunk of flesh from its large prey.

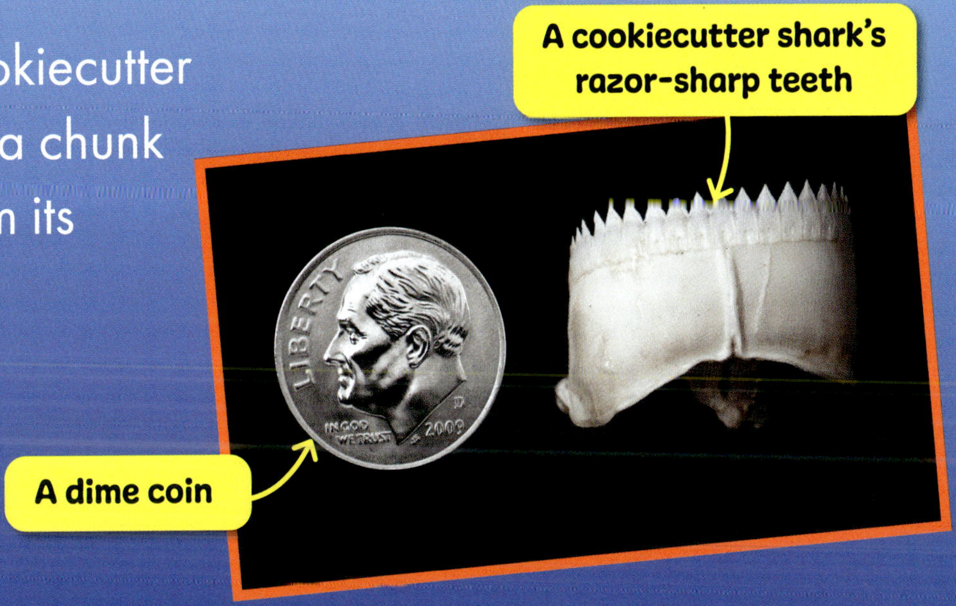

The bite looks like it's been made by a cookie cutter!

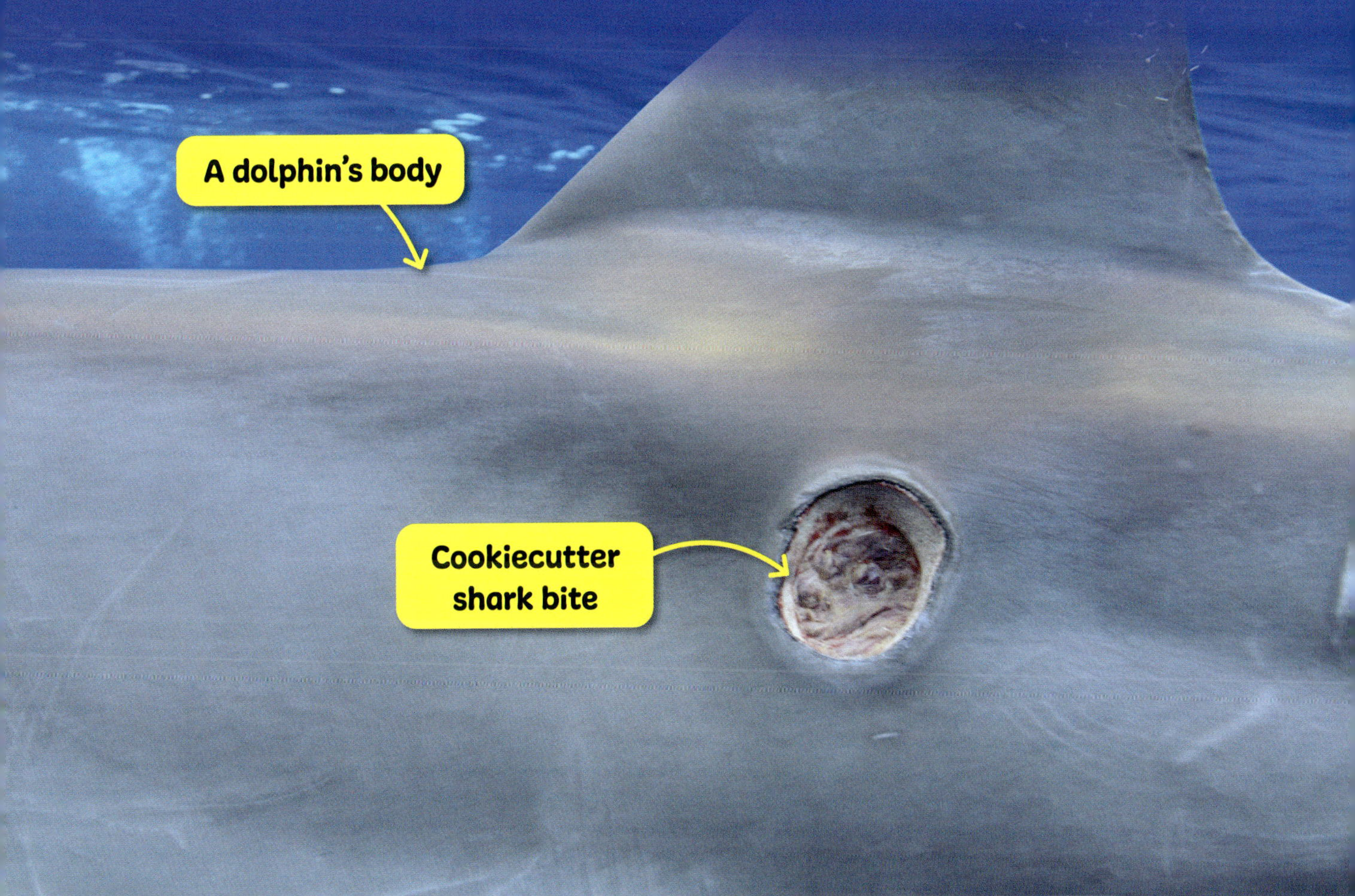

Bites from cookiecutter sharks can be seen on whales, dolphins, seals, and fish.

Do Sharks Have Cousins?

Skates and rays are close fishy relatives of sharks. They have flat bodies and long tails.

Some rays can sting with their tails!

These eagle rays use their fins like wings.

These shark cousins are guitarfish, or shovelnose rays. They bury themselves in the sand.

When a crab, shrimp, or fish passes by, they pounce at high speed!

Just like sharks, skates and rays have skeletons made of cartilage and skin covered with denticles.

Which Ray Is a Giant?

It's the incredible giant manta ray. It's the biggest ray in the world.

The word *manta* is Spanish for "blanket."

This huge ray swims by flapping its massive wing-like fins.

Manta rays eat small fish and zooplankton.

Manta rays visit underwater fishy places known as cleaning stations.

Small fish pick parasites off the skin of bigger fish—and get a free meal.

How Do Sharks Have Babies?

There are three ways that sharks have their young.

Some types of sharks give birth to live babies.

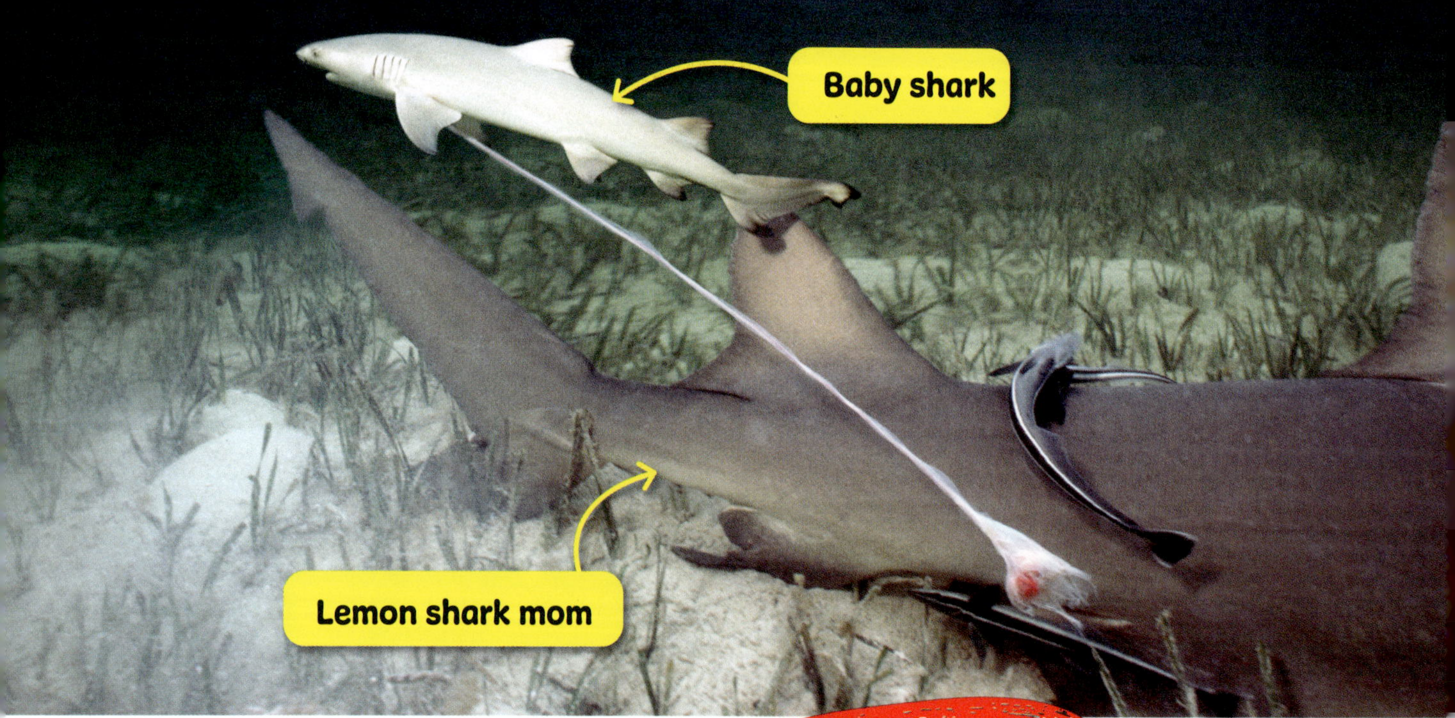

Some sharks lay an egg inside an egg case.

A pup hatches from the egg.

A Port Jackson shark egg case

Some pups, such as great white sharks, hatch from eggs inside their moms.

Then their mom gives birth to them.

Scientists studying a great white shark pup

What Is a Mermaid's Purse?

Have you ever found something that looks like this washed up on a beach?

People used to think they were tiny lost purses that mermaids used for their treasures.

It is known as a mermaid's purse!

They are the empty egg cases of skates, rays, and some types of sharks.

It takes 12 months for a swell shark to grow and be ready to hatch.

Do Shark Pups Go to Nurseries?

Yes! Some shark pups live in safe places called nurseries.

Shark moms come to these habitats to give birth.

Mangroves are warm habitats with shallow water.

There are lots of thick, twisted tree roots.

Little shark pups can hide in a mangrove from predators, such as bigger sharks.

Lemon shark pups grow slowly.

They stay in a mangrove nursery for about seven years.

Why Do Sharks Go Traveling?

Sharks travel to find food, places to have their pups, and warmer waters.

Bronze whaler sharks migrate to follow sardines.

Great white sharks migrate to feed on their favorite food—seals.

Blue sharks travel to nurseries to give birth.

A blue shark may give birth to 35 pups at one time!

Hammerhead sharks like to live in warm water.

If the water gets too cold, they migrate to a warmer place.

Should People Be Scared of Sharks?

When people enter a shark's habitat, they should be careful.

Sharks are hunters that eat other animals.

A shark might make a mistake and think a person is its prey.

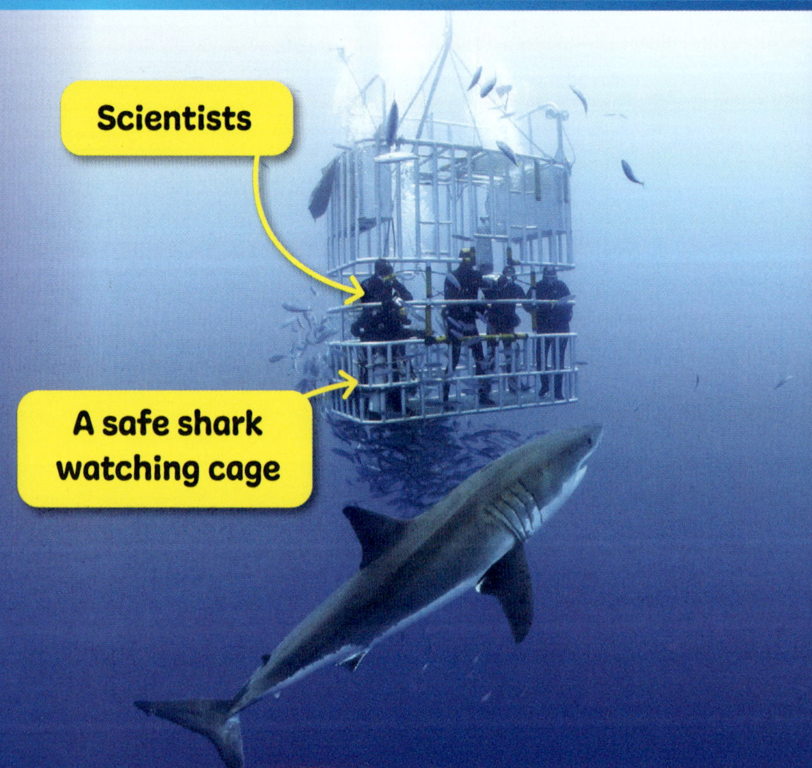

Only a few sharks, such as bull and tiger sharks, have attacked people.

Sharks actually have more to fear from people.

Millions of sharks are killed each year!

Shark fins

Shark fin soup

Their fins are used to make shark fin soup.

What Does a Shark Scientist Do?

Shark scientists study these amazing animals to discover how they live.

Shark scientists measure and weigh sharks, and record the information.

Sharks are fitted with **tracking devices**.

They tell scientists where sharks go and how far they travel.

Sometimes scientists help rescue injured or trapped sharks.

How Do Shark Scientists Stay Safe?

When scientists need to study sharks underwater, they have lots of ways to stay safe.

Scientists dive in groups so they can look out for each other.

They avoid splashing, because sharks are attracted to splashing prey.

Scientists don't wear jewelry and watches because sharks are attracted to shiny objects.

This scientist is wearing a special wetsuit.

It keeps sharks from sensing electrical signals.

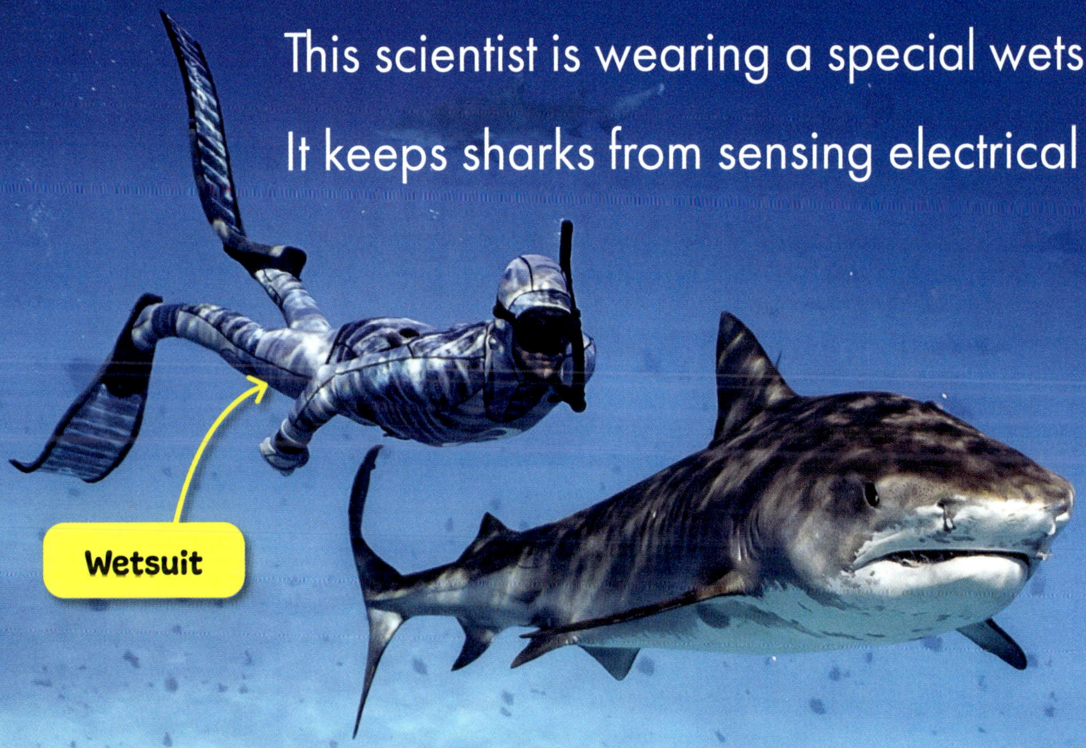

Scientists look out for warning signs that a shark may be about to attack.

How Smart Are Sharks?

Sharks are smart animals.
They use their brain power for hunting.

Nurse sharks have learned to stand and walk on their fins.

Scientists think this body position helps them grab at food on the seabed.

This pack of gray reef sharks are following a scent in the water.

They've learned it's easier to find prey if they use teamwork.

Sharks use their bodies to talk to other sharks.

They may open their jaws or arch their back.

Why Are Sharks So Important?

Oceans need just the right amount of animals and plants.

If too many plant-eaters feed on seagrass, they might damage the underwater meadows.

Sharks hunt and scare away turtles and other seagrass munchers.

Sharks hunt the big fish that eat smaller fish.

This helps keep just the right amount of fish in the ocean.

Sharks help clean up by eating dead and diseased animals.

Why Are Sharks in Danger?

Sharks face many dangers!

Plastic trash and other pollution get washed out to sea.

Sharks may eat plastic trash.

Plastic can get wrapped around a shark's body and hurt it.

Sharks can die if they get caught in fishing nets.

Too much shark fishing means fewer sharks.

Some people sell shark jaws and teeth as **souvenirs**.

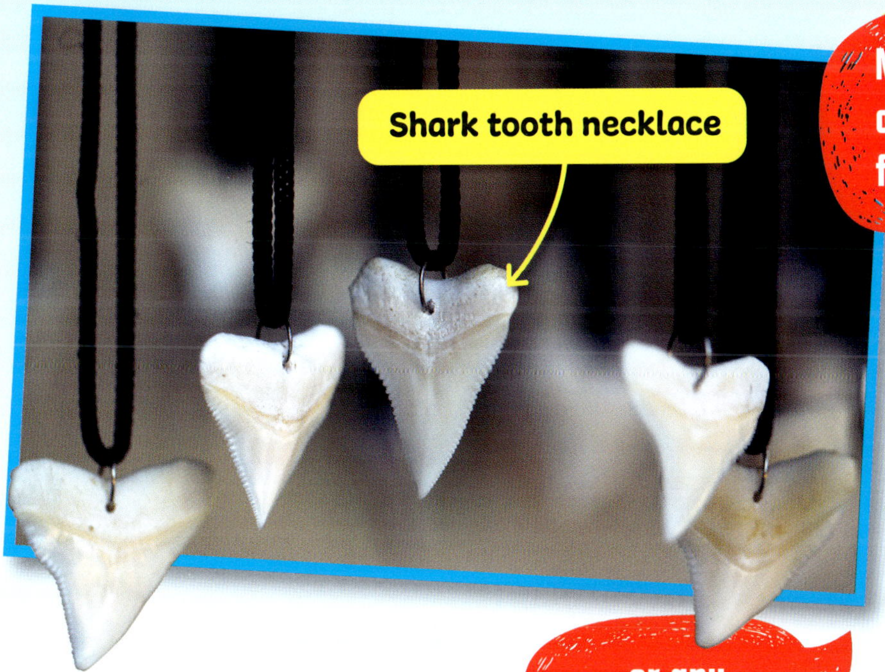

How Can You Help Sharks?

Learn all you can about sharks. You can make a BIG difference!

Protect the Ocean

Plastic on beaches can be washed out to sea. Ask if you can do a beach clean-up.

Cleaning up near a river is good, too, because rivers flow out to sea.

Adopt a Shark

You can pay a small amount of money to a shark charity to adopt a shark.

The money helps scientists study and protect sharks.

Use Your Voice!

These protestors want people to stop eating shark fin soup.

Snappy Super-Facts

If you were to touch a shark, its skin would feel rough, like sandpaper.

Some sharks may have 30,000 teeth in their life! New teeth are always growing to replace the ones that fall out.

Sharks DO NOT eat people. Shark attacks happen when sharks make a mistake and think a person is their prey.

Sharks can go without food for weeks or months.

Basking sharks give birth to the biggest shark babies. A pup can be more than 5 feet (1.5 m) long!

You have body parts called vocal cords that help you talk. Sharks can't make sounds because they don't have vocal cords.

Bonnethead sharks nibble on seagrass. Scientists don't know why they do this.

Shark Awareness Day is on July 14. It's a day for talking about the importance of sharks.

Sharks eat sharks! Smaller sharks are eaten by bigger sharks.

Some shark pups eat their brothers and sisters inside their mom before they are born.

Lemon sharks make friends. They choose other lemon sharks who they like to hang out with—just like you make friends!

Sharks can sense their prey's heartbeat. That's because hearts give off electrical signals.

Swell sharks really do swell up! They gulp in water to make their bodies bigger if they are threatened.

The largest great white shark recorded was 20 feet (6 m) long.

My Shark Words

camouflage
Colors or patterns on an animal's body that help it blend into its background or habitat.

carnivore
An animal that only eats meat.

cartilage
The light, bendy material that makes up a shark's skeleton.

characteristic
A feature or quality that you can notice. For example, a big mouth or spotted skin are characteristics of some sharks.

cold-blooded
When an animal's body temperature matches the temperature of the air or water around it.

coral reef
A rock-like ocean habitat made up of the shells of tiny animals called corals. Many animals live on coral reefs.

denticles
Small, hard, v-shaped scales on a shark's skin.

extinct
No longer alive and gone forever.

filter
To sieve, or remove, something from water.

fin
A body part of water animals such as fish and whales.

fossil
The rocky remains of an animal or plant that lived millions of years ago.

gills
Body parts that sharks and other fish use for breathing. Gills take in oxygen from water.

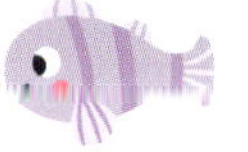

habitat
A natural place where an animal lives, finds its food, and finds mates. The ocean is a type of habitat.

oxygen
A gas in the air that animals and people need to breathe.

parasite
A living thing that lives on or in another living thing and feeds on it.

plankton
Very tiny animals and plant-like living things that drift in oceans, lakes, rivers, and ponds.

pollution
Trash, smoke, chemicals, or other bad substances that can make water, air, and the land dirty and unsafe.

predator
An animal that hunts other animals for food.

prehistoric
A long, long time ago before people began recording history.

prey
An animal that is hunted by other animals for food.

souvenir
An item a person buys or keeps to remind them of something special, such as a vacation.

tracking device
A small device that's attached to an animal. It sends information to scientists—for example, where a shark travels.

Big Shark Quiz

1: Which living shark is the biggest?
- a] Whale shark
- b] Elephant shark
- c] Tiger shark

2: What do sharks use to breathe?
- a] Teeth
- b] Fins
- c] Gills

3: What is a shark's skeleton made of?
- a] Bone
- b] Cartilage
- c] Rubber

4: What is a mermaid's purse?
- a] A tiny bag
- b] An empty egg case
- c] A type of seashell

5: Which shark is the biggest of all time?
- a] Megalotooth
- b] Megalofin
- c] Megalodon

6: Which shark can live for 400 years?
- a] Greenland shark
- b] Salmon shark
- c] Basking shark

7: Which of these sharks feasts on krill?
- a] Great white shark
- b] Megamouth shark
- c] Mako shark

8: What are shark babies called?
- a] Kits
- b] Calves
- c] Pups

9: Which shark can live in rivers?
- a] Horn shark
- b] Bull shark
- c] Reef shark

10: How long have sharks been around?
- a] 450 million years
- b] 450 years
- c] 50 years

Answers:
1]a 2]c 3]b 4]b 5]c 6]a 7]b 8]c 9]b 10]a